Book Designed, Organized, and Illustrated by Brijae Morris

Book Edited by Dr. jill moniz

www.brijaemorris.com

ISBN-13: 978-1984096333

Cover Illustration: Aida Overton Walker as *Salome*, 1912, in Oscar Hammerstein's revival of the Richard Strauss opera

For Aida

Foreward

I found **Aida Overton Walker** in my last year of college at Otis College of Art and Design. Every year the senior class creates a school-wide art show to demonstrate everything they have learned. Years before my own show, I would periodically think of what my project would be and how it would directly represent me. When I attended other senior shows at Otis, I never saw natural hair on black women. As a black woman with natural hair, I decided to dedicate my year-long project to giving this reality a voice and point of view that was previously absent at Otis College.

I started my project by researching natural hair, and through that process, the direction of my project turned into a brief history of natural hair in America. I wanted the viewer to understand every intention, significance, and emotion behind a black woman's hair. My historical research continued and when I reached the Victorian Era, I stumbled upon the amazing Aida Overton Walker.

My first thought was I have *never* seen a black Victorian woman so adorned with jewels in every photograph. I knew she had to be someone important, but I couldn't say why. Doing what anyone would do in my position, I did a quick Google search and was completely astonished that I have never heard of this wonderful woman who dedicated her entire life to a beautiful art form. It made no sense to me how Aida Overton Walker has been forgotten to history. She was so well known and revered during her lifetime that there is no reason the same couldn't be said for after.

The more I learned about Mrs. Walker the more I wanted her story to be told to everyone who has been denied the privilege of knowing her. Making it my personal mission to retell her story to a new generation, this book is entirely in honor of Aida Overton Walker, George Walker, and all the black entertainers who have to overcome stereotypes to simply do what they love.

-Brijae Morris

Her Story

Originally named Ada Wilman Overton, she was born in New York, on February 14, 1880, Valentine's Day. She was the second child of Pauline Whitfield, a seamstress and Moses Overton, a waiter. Always dancing at home, her parents had her receive a formal dance education from Mrs. Thorp. Working hard and excelling, Ada graduated from Thorp's Dance School in 1897.

A friend invited Ada to model for an advertisement with Bert Williams and George W. Walker, who had just scored a hit with their vaudeville debut at Koster & Bial's Music Hall. Ada agreed to model for the ad, and from there, their personal and professioal relationship blossomed.

Together, Ada Overton, George W. Walker, and Bert Williams joined Black Patti's Troubadours in 1896, where their 'cakewalk' gained nation-wide popularity. The cakewalk dance developed in the late 19th century after emacipation from the 'prize walks' held at get togethers by former black slaves. The dance got its name from a competition at the 1876 Centennial Exposition in Philadelphia where a large cake would be presented to the winning couple.

As Ada explained it,

"The cakewalk is characteristic of a race and in order to understand it and appreciate it and to become adept in it, it is necessary to keep your mind upon the judges, your partner, and especially upon what the cakewalk really is—a gala dance..."

Illustration: c. 1900

Tom Fletcher, a fellow black vaudeville entertainer, remembered that Ada Overton was a dancer "who could do almost anything, and no matter whether it was a buck-and-wing, cakewalk, or even some form of grotesque dancing, she lent the performance a neat gracefulness of movement which was unsurpassed by anyone."

Ada continued to shine and promptly joined the cast of John W. Isham's Octroons when they performed at the Bowery Theatre on September 6, 1897, when Ada was only 17 years old.

Within a short time of their collaboration, Ada Overton and George Walker married on June 22, 1899. They became the leading cakewalking couple in the new century. With Bert Williams, the couple toured with their namesake The Walker and Williams Company.

Through The Walker and Williams Company, Ada, George and Bert immediately began producing shows, the first being *The Policy Players* in 1899.

Ada also appeared in *Sons of Ham*, playing the character Miss Hannah from Savannah in 1900. In her rendition, Ada won praise for combining superb vocal control with acting skill that together presented a positive, strong image of black womanhood. Ada quickly found her next prestigious role, *In Dahomey* in 1902. In this production, the famous cakewalk dance began to transform with a new direction developed within the company. Ada reinterpreted the low-down cakewalk into an elegant dance, making it her signature dance. Her stardom and cakewalking fame helped open the door to new opportunities making the cakewalk a respectable dance form.

Illustration: Aida and George Walker, *In Dahomey*, 1903

With her popularity growing as dancer, choreographer, comedienne and singer, Ada soon changed the spelling of her name from Ada to Aida, the name of the Haitian loa (spirit) of fertility, rainbows, snakes, and the wife of snake god Danbala. Walker knew her performances as a black woman were entirely unique and were interpreted differently than the performances of a white woman. By embracing her new name, Aida Overton Walker made no measure to hide her black identity.

The Walker and Williams Company was invited to Europe for two seasons in 1904. Aida appeared before King Edward of England at Buckingham Palace. Even with her growing success, Aida Overton Walker never lost sight of the fact that in the eyes of many she represented something more.

Aida was frequently contracted by the leading elite hostesses of New York, London, and Paris to instruct guests in the mysteries of the popular cakewalk dance that had originated among black slaves on Southern plantations.

In a 1905 Colored American article, Walker is clear in the belief that the performing arts could have an effect on race relations, stating that "I venture to think and dare to state that our profession does more toward the alleviation of color prejudice than any other profession among colored people."

When Aida returned to America, the Vanderbilt family of Newport, Rhode Island hired The Walker and Williams Company to entertain their guests at salaries of a $1,000 dollars each. Aida performed and was also welcomed as a guest.

At this point Aida was the highest paid and most popular female actress, singer, and dancer of The Walker and Williams Company. The Walker couple were in a class of exceedingly few, compared to most blacks; they owned a private car, beautiful clothes and expensive jewels. Mrs. Walker's diamond necklace could be converted into a tiara. This indicated the potential and possibility for mobility among African Americans during a time where the average working household in New York made $675 dollars a year.

Illustration: c. 1911

The Walker and Williams company continued to produce extremely successful shows, namely *Abyssinia* in 1906 and *Bandanna Land* in 1908, when Aida Overton Walker first choreographed her own version of the *Salome* dance. Williams saw the *Salome* craze and integrated burlesque into Aida's dances, positioning her as a modern dancer.

It was received with mixed reviews. Critics emphasized her modest costume and gracefulness, as well as the lack of vulgarity, contrary to the dance's traditional characteristics. Aida highlighted the dramatized elements instead of the suggestive. She recognized how the roles she played on stage would effect her race and worked hard to break stereotypes of black women and actresses as immoral and oversexualized.

She said, "I am aware of the fact than many well-meaning people dislike stage life, especially our women. On that point, I'd say, a woman doesn't have to lose her dignity."

Aida Overton Walker's dances were less entertainment and more artistry. Rather than showing off her body, Walker conveyed her imagination and emotional conviction as an expression of her values and artistic ideas.

Illustration: c. 1907

In late 1908, George Walker suddenly collapsed during the tour of *Bandanna Land*. He was later diagnosed with syphilis. He left the show in 1908 and his role was rewritten for Aida, who donned his flashy male clothes and sang his numbers. She successfully performed the male role, expanding the narrow societal view for women on stage. *Bandanna Land* eventually ran its course and had its last show in 1909.

While renewing her contract with The Walker and Williams Company, Aida joined the cast of Bob Cole and J. Rosamand Johnson's *Red Moon*, and she was featured in two numbers: *Pheobe Brown* and *Pickaninny Days*. She next opened at the American Theater in 1909 with a vaudeville act featuring herself and eight girls of color.

In 1910, Aida established the Smart Set Company, becoming the leader of her own vaudeville production, and distanced herself from The Walker and Williams Company after her husband left to recover from his poor health. During this time she also began touring the vaudeville circuit as a solo act.

On January 8, 1911 her husband of twelve years died from his illness. George Walker was buried at Oak Hill Cemetery, in his hometown of Lawrence, Kansas. Fulfilling his role of a race leader rather than that of just an entertainer, George Walker made many significant contributions through his productions and the management of The Walker and Williams Company.

In 1911, after a brief mourning period Aida Overton Walker started performing the new production *His Honor the Barber* with the Smart Set Company. Although she was billed as a supporting actress, the press would remember her as S. H. Dudely's costar. Both critics and the audience were more than impressed with her work, and her performances were very well received. She sang the male lead *Shine*, honoring her late husband. According to Perry Bradford, a songster and publisher, the song was written about an actual man named Shine who was with George Walker when they were badly beaten during the 1900 New York City race riot.

Illustration: Aida and George Walker

By 1912, Aida effectively cut all ties to The Walker and Williams Company, and was free of Bert Williams, who undermined her vision. Aida headlined her own vaudeville act on a 16-week tour through the Midwest. She appeared at the Majestic Theatre and Chicago's Pekin Theatre, which was the first black owned musical and vaudeville stock theatre in the United States. The performance was so popular it was extended to November 3, 1913. It was said that the house was full every night to catch a glimpse of the famous Aida Overton Walker. When Aida returned from her long tour, she was invited by Oscar Hammerstein to perform her *Salome* dance at his Roof Garden Theatre (Victoria Theatre) on Broadway.

From 1912 until 1914, Aida continued to choreograph numbers for two black female dance groups: the Happy Girls and Porto Rico Girls, whose dancers included Lottie Gee, who would later star in the musical revue *Shuffle Along* in 1921, and Elida Webb, who would star at the Cotton Club in the 1920s. Aida encouraged the girls to create original dance routines and insisted that they dress in stylish costumes on stage, giving them a sense of professionalism.

Aida continued performing at Hammerstein's until two months before her death. On October 11, 1914, Aida Overton Walker suddenly died from kidney failure. She was only 34 years old. Her obituary in *The Freeman* newspaper claimed that Aida suffered a nervous breakdown a week prior to her shocking and unexpected death.

As Aida was one of the first international black performers, the African American entertainment community in New York went into deep mourning following her death. The *New York Age* featured a lengthy obituary on its front page. Hundreds of shocked and saddened entertainers descended on her Harlem home, a brick and brownstone row house at 107 West 132nd Street, to confirm a story they hoped was untrue. In Aida, fellow performers and the world lost the greatest female entertainer of their time.

Aida Overton Walker's interest in both African American indigenous material and her translation of these cultural legacies to the modern stage anticipated the choreographic work of modern dance pioneers to come.

Constance Valis Hill detailed that both in Aida's solo work for women and in the unison and precision choreographies for the female chorus, Aida claimed a female presence on the American theatrical stage. By negotiating the narrow white definitions of appropriate black performances with her own version of black specialization and innovation, Aida established an onstage black cultural identity that created a model by which African American musical artists could gain acceptance worldwide.

In addition to her attractive stage persona and highly acclaimed performances, Aida won the hearts of fellow African American entertainers, performing numerous benefits near the end of her tragically short career, and for her cultivation of young women performers.

She was, in the words of the New York Age's Lester Walton, the exponent of "clean, refined artistic entertainment."

Many historians agree that Aida was only just reaching the height of her career at the time of her death. Thousands passed her bier at St. Philip's Episcopal Church in New York to cast their final gaze on 'The Queen of the Cakewalk'. The famous Aida Overton Walker is buried in Brooklyn at Cypress Hills Cemetery Plot Section 15, Locust Grove, Block 16, Division 2, Grave 12811.

"Unless we learn the lesson of self-appreciation and practice it,

we shall spend our lives imitating other people and deprecating our-selves."

-Aida Overton Walker

Sources

"1901 (From "100 Years of US Consumer Spending")."
U.S. Department of Labor, U.S. Bureau of Labor Statistics, www.bls.gov/opub/uscs/1901.pdf.

Adams, Michael H. "Aida Overton Walker, 'Bobbie' Hargous and Why All That's 'Gilded' Is Hardly Golden!" Mr. Michael Henry Adams' Style & Taste, 27 Dec. 2017, http://mrmhadams.typepad.com/blog/2013/12/why-all-thats-gilded-is-hardly-golden.html

"Aida Overton Walker." Find a Grave. Accessed December 26, 2017. https://www.findagrave.com/cgi-bin/fg.cgi?page=gr&GRid=115047819

Altman, Susan. "Entertainer, Aida Overton Walker." Entertainer, Aida Overton Walker , 1997, www.aaregistry.org/historic_events/view/entertainer-aida-overton-walker.

Baldwin, Brooke (1981). "The Cakewalk: A Study in Stereotype and Reality". Journal of Social History. Oxford University Press. 15 (2): 205–218. doi:10.1353/jsh/15.2.205. ISSN 0022-4529. JSTOR 3787107.

Brown, Jayna. Babylon Girls: Black Women Performers and the Shaping of the Modern. Durham: Duke University Press, 2008.

"Gender-Bending on Stage: The Power of Play." Acrocollective.net, 5 Mar. 2016, acrocollective.net/2015/04/11/gender-bending-theatre-performance/.

Hill, Constance. "Ada Overton Walker." *American Memory from the Library of Congress,* memory.loc.gov/diglib/ihas/loc.music.tdabio.182/default.html.

Krasner, David. A Beautiful Pageant: African American Theater Drama and Performance in the Harlem Renaissance 1910-1927. New York: Palgrave Macmillan, 2002.

Morgan, Thomas L. "Cecil Mack – R. C. McPherson". Jazz Roots. Retrieved 22 Dec. 2017.

Russell, Sylvester. "Aida Overton Walker Passes Away at Twilight at Her Home in New York City." *The Freeman*, 17 Oct. 1914, pp. 5–5.

Sotiropoulos, Karen. Staging Race : Black Performers in Turn of the Century America. Cambridge, MA, USA: Harvard University Press, 2006. ProQuest ebrary. Web. 27 Dec. 2017. Copyright © 2006. Harvard University Press.

"Walker, Aida Overton (1880-1914)." St. James Encyclopedia of Popular Culture. *Encyclopedia.com*. 20 Dec. 2017, http://www.encyclopedia.com.

Walton, Lester A. "A LIVING INFLUENCE." *The New York Age*, 22 Oct. 1914, pp. 6–6.

Printed in Great Britain
by Amazon

27839457R00018